AF270413

PITTSBURGH PIRATES

BY PATRICK DONNELLY

SportsZone

An Imprint of Abdo Publishing
abdobooks.com

abdobooks.com

Published by Abdo Publishing, a division of ABDO, PO Box 398166, Minneapolis, Minnesota 55439. Copyright © 2023 by Abdo Consulting Group, Inc. International copyrights reserved in all countries. No part of this book may be reproduced in any form without written permission from the publisher. SportsZone™ is a trademark and logo of Abdo Publishing.

Printed in China.
102022
012023

Cover Photo: Gene J. Puskar/AP Images
Interior Photos: Jonathan Daniel/Getty Images Sport/Getty Images, 4; Mark Rucker/ Transcendental Graphics/Getty Images Sport/Getty Images, 7, 9, 11, 13, 20; George Rinhart/Corbis Historical/Getty Images, 14; Bettmann/Getty Images, 16, 22; Bruce Bennett/Getty Images, 18; Focus on Sport/Getty Images Sport/Getty Images, 25, 35; Bruce Bennett Studios/Getty Images Studio/Getty Images, 26; George Gojkovich/Getty Images Sport/Getty Images, 28; Focus on Sport/Getty Images, 30, 32; Ron Vesely/MLB/ Getty Images Sport/Getty Images, 37; Rich Pilling/MLB/Getty Images, 39; Justin K. Aller/ Getty Images Sport/Getty Images, 40; Justin Berl/Getty Images Sport/Getty Images, 41

Editor: Steph Giedd
Series Designer: Becky Daum

Library of Congress Control Number: 2022940489

Publisher's Cataloging-in-Publication Data

Names: Donnelly, Patrick, author.
Title: Pittsburgh Pirates / by Patrick Donnelly
Description: Minneapolis, Minnesota: Abdo Publishing, 2023 | Series: Inside MLB | Includes online resources and index.
Identifiers: ISBN 9781098290290 (lib. bdg.) | ISBN 9781098275495 (ebook)
Subjects: LCSH: Pittsburgh Pirates (Baseball team)--Juvenile literature. | Baseball teams--Juvenile literature. | Professional sports--Juvenile literature. | Sports franchises--Juvenile literature. | Major League Baseball (Organization)--Juvenile literature.
Classification: DDC 796.35764--dc23

TABLE OF CONTENTS

CHAPTER 1

BECOMING THE PIRATES

On August 29, 2021, the visiting St. Louis Cardinals led the last-place Pittsburgh Pirates 3–1. Alex Reyes, the Cardinals' hard-throwing closer, came in to finish the game. But the Pirates began to rally.

Yoshi Tsutsugo faced Reyes with two runners on base and one out. The Pirates had signed the Japanese outfielder just 13 days earlier. In that short time, he had hit four home runs for his new team. Fans watching the game questioned whether Tsutsugo could do it again.

It didn't take long for him to answer. On the first pitch, Reyes tried to sneak a breaking ball past Tsutsugo. But it wasn't a sharp pitch. The ball spun and hung over home plate.

Slugger Yoshi Tsutsugo hit 8 homers and 25 runs batted in (RBIs) in his first season with the Pirates, despite joining late in the season.

Tsutsugo lashed at it with a powerful left-handed swing, and the ball took off. The crowd erupted in cheers. The ball was headed high and deep to right field. There was no doubt it was a game-winning home run for Tsutsugo.

The ball didn't just carry over the fence. It left the ballpark entirely, clearing the right-field seats and heading toward the Allegheny River, which borders Pittsburgh's PNC Park. The three-run homer gave the Pirates a 4–3 victory.

As Tsutsugo trotted around the bases, his teammates gathered at home plate. When he arrived, they mobbed him, sprayed water on him, and jumped around in celebration. It might have been a bad year overall for the Pirates. But moments like this one gave the players and their fans reason for hope.

MEET THE ALLEGHENYS

The Pittsburgh Alleghenys brought professional baseball to Pittsburgh in 1877. They were named for the mountain region in western Pennsylvania. The Alleghenys were a minor league team, and they lasted only two years.

Four years later, a new version of the Alleghenys was born. This team competed in the American Association (AA). That was a rival to the more established National League (NL), which was founded in 1876.

The 1889 Pittsburgh Alleghenys featured four future Hall of Famers, including Pud Galvin, *middle row, far left*.

The Alleghenys spent five seasons in the AA. Their best season came in 1886, when they finished in second place, 12 games behind the champion St. Louis Browns. Their top players were both starting pitchers. Ed Morris, a 23-year-old lefty, won 41 games and threw a league-high 12 shutouts. Meanwhile, future Hall of Famer James Francis "Pud" Galvin won 29 games.

In baseball's early days, the makeup of the various leagues was a bit more fluid than it is today. It wasn't uncommon for a team to switch from the AA to the NL, especially as other teams went out of business. In 1886 a team called the Kansas City Cowboys joined the NL and promptly went 30–91 in their first season. It turned out to be their only one. The Cowboys went out of business, and their spot in the NL was filled by the Alleghenys.

The emergence of another rival league would give Pittsburgh's team a new and more lasting nickname. In 1890 the Players League was formed. The new league raided the rosters of clubs from the AA and the NL to build their teams. The Alleghenys lost a lot of their key players and finished last in the NL with a 23–113 record.

However, the Players League folded after just one season. Its players were expected to rejoin their former clubs in 1891. Most of them did. But infielder Lou Bierbauer, who had previously played for the AA's Philadelphia Athletics, didn't return to Philadelphia. He signed with Pittsburgh instead. The AA clubs were furious at Pittsburgh and said the team had "pirated" one of their players. The Alleghenys liked the sound of that, and the team became known as the Pittsburgh Pirates in 1891.

The Pirates weren't much of a threat during the 1890s, usually finishing in the middle of the pack of the 12-team NL. But in 1900, the NL cut back to an eight-team league, dumping teams from Baltimore, Cleveland, Louisville, and Washington, DC. The owner of the Louisville club, Barney Dreyfuss, bought the Pirates. And he brought 14 of his old players with him, including future Hall of Famers Honus Wagner and Fred Clarke.

That addition of talent turned the Pirates into instant contenders. They finished in second place in 1900. Then, in 1901, the American League (AL) was founded. Its eight teams signed away many

Hall of Fame shortstop Honus Wagner led the majors in doubles and triples in his first season with Pittsburgh.

talented players from NL clubs. But the Pirates largely stuck together, and that made them an NL power in the early 1900s. They won three straight league titles starting in 1901, with Wagner emerging as a superstar. He led the league in runs batted in (RBIs) and stolen bases in 1901 and 1902. Meanwhile,

HONUS WAGNER

One of the greatest hitters in baseball history was a Pittsburgh native who spent 18 seasons with his hometown team. Defensively, Honus Wagner played all over the diamond before settling in at shortstop. But he made a name for himself with his bat. Wagner won eight NL batting titles and retired in 1917 with 3,420 hits. More than a century later, that still put him among the top 10 in baseball history.

Clarke served as manager while also playing the outfield and hitting .330 over that three-year span.

In January 1903, the leaders of the AL and NL agreed to cooperate with each other and stop signing each other's players. This new arrangement created the basic structure of baseball that we know today. It also opened the door for the possibility of a postseason meeting of the leagues' champions for the first time. That August, the Pirates and the Boston Americans had big leads in their respective leagues. Dreyfuss challenged Henry Killilea, owner of the Americans, to a postseason series if each team finished in first. And that's exactly what happened.

The first "Championship of the United States"—later known as the World Series—began on October 1, 1903. It was a series of nine games, meaning the champion would be the first team to win five games. The Pirates took three of the first four games. But Boston then rallied to win four straight and took the series 5–3.

The Pittsburgh Pirates played at Forbes Field from 1909 to 1970.

A NEW HOME

Pittsburgh remained competitive but didn't win another pennant until 1909. That summer the Pirates also opened a new ballpark. They had played home games at Exposition Park since 1891. The old stadium's wooden grandstands were a fire hazard. And its location on the banks of the Allegheny River led to frequent flooding. Forbes Field, located just outside of downtown Pittsburgh, was one of the first modern ballparks, built with steel and concrete. It opened on June 30, 1909, with a 3–2 loss to the defending champion Chicago Cubs.

The Pirates didn't suffer many losses that year, however. They went 110–42, winning the league by 6.5 games over the Cubs. At 35 years old, Wagner was still playing like a man in his prime. He hit .339 to win his fourth straight NL batting title. He also led the league with 39 doubles and 100 RBIs. The Pirates' pitching ace was right-hander Howie Camnitz, who went 25–6 with a 1.62 earned-run average (ERA).

In the World Series, the Pirates faced the Detroit Tigers, winners of their third straight AL crown. The Tigers were led by 22-year-old center fielder Ty Cobb, who hit .377 that season to win the third of his record 12 AL batting titles. Pittsburgh's pitchers held Cobb in check, however, limiting him to just six hits in the seven-game series. Rookie pitcher Babe Adams won three games for Pittsburgh, including a six-hit shutout in Game 7. That 8–0 victory gave the Pirates their first World Series title.

Pittsburgh star Honus Wagner, *right*, poses with Detroit Tigers great Ty Cobb before Game 3 of the 1909 World Series.

FROM KIKI TO CLEMENTE

After their World Series win, the Pirates returned to the middle of the pack before hitting rock bottom in 1917. That year they went 51–103 to finish in last place in the NL. To make matters worse, it was Honus Wagner's final season as a player. The 43-year-old still managed to hit .265 in 73 games. Wagner collected his final career hit, a single off the Cincinnati Reds' Joe Engel, on September 3, 1917.

Those Pittsburgh teams of the late 1910s weren't without stars, however. Babe Adams, the 1909 World Series hero, carved out a strong career with the Pirates. His rookie year was the first of 10 seasons in which Adams posted at least 10 wins with an ERA below 3.00. Meanwhile, center fielder Max Carey

Pirates speedster Max Carey led the NL in stolen bases 10 times between 1913 and 1925.

Hall of Fame center fielder Kiki Cuyler played seven of his 18 seasons with the Pirates.

developed into one of the top speedsters of his era. Carey led the NL in stolen bases 10 times between 1913 and 1925 and retired with an NL record 738 career steals.

Both players stuck around long enough to see the Pirates turn things around. The next wave of stars began arriving in Pittsburgh in the early 1920s. Rookie Pie Traynor won the third base job in 1922 and went on to a Hall of Fame career. Center fielder Kiki Cuyler, another future Hall of Famer, cracked the starting lineup in 1924.

The pieces came together in 1925, when the Pirates slugged their way to the NL pennant. They led the league with a team batting average of .307. Much to the dismay of opposing pitchers, there wasn't a weak spot in the Pirates' lineup. Seven of their eight starters hit .300 or better that year. The only

exception, second baseman Eddie Moore, finished with a
.298 average.

They weren't just slap hitters, either. Pittsburgh led the
majors in doubles and triples. And when they got on base, the
trouble was just beginning. The Pirates also led the league in
stolen bases. Cuyler had an amazing season, posting a .357
average and a league-high 26 triples. Carey hit .343 and swiped
46 bases, five more than Cuyler.

BATTLING THE BIG TRAIN

The Pirates faced the Washington Senators in the 1925 World
Series. The Senators were another strong hitting club. And
Washington legend Walter "Big Train" Johnson was still working
his magic on the mound at age 37. Washington jumped out
to a quick lead, winning three of the first four games. But
the Pirates rallied to win the next two, forcing a decisive
showdown at Forbes Field.

Game 7 started on a worrying note for Pittsburgh. The
Senators knocked out Pirates starter Vic Aldridge with four
runs in the top of the first. Washington felt confident with the
Big Train on the mound in a do-or-die game, but the Pirates
wouldn't give in. They chipped away at Johnson, eventually
cutting the Senators' lead to 7–6 entering the bottom of
the eighth.

Though the Pirates struck out Yankees star Babe Ruth in this at-bat, New York went on to win the 1927 World Series in a sweep.

Johnson retired the first two batters, but Earl Smith and Carson Bigbee hit back-to-back doubles to tie the game. A walk and an error loaded the bases, bringing up Cuyler. He lashed a ball to right field that rolled into foul territory and under the bullpen tarp. Ruled a ground-rule double, the hit drove in two runs. And when reliever Red Oldham retired the Senators in order in the ninth, Pittsburgh had a 9–7 victory and its second World Series title.

The Pirates made it back to the World Series in 1927, but they ran into a buzzsaw called the New York Yankees. The 1927 Yankees were one of the greatest hitting teams of all time. Anchored by sluggers Babe Ruth and Lou Gehrig, the Yankees crushed their AL opponents, winning 110 games. They had little trouble with the Pirates in the World Series, finishing them off with a four-game sweep.

A LONG DRY SPELL

Pirates fans would have to savor those two pennants, because it would be more than three decades before they'd see another World Series at Forbes Field. Still, they got to watch some great players along the way. Paul Waner and his brother, Lloyd, were known as "Big Poison" and "Little Poison," respectively. The Waners patrolled the Pittsburgh outfield together from 1927 to 1940. They combined for 5,611 career hits and became the first brothers elected to the Baseball Hall of Fame as players.

The Pirates' offensive attack got a jolt of power with the arrival of 23-year-old Ralph Kiner in 1946. That came just after the end of World War II (1939–1945). After spending three years serving in the military, Kiner hit the ground running—or rather, swinging—as a rookie. He won the NL title with 23 homers that year. He bashed 51 home runs to lead the major leagues the next year. And he just kept swinging for the fences. In all, Kiner won seven straight major league home run titles. In 1949 he hit 54 to become the first NL player to top 50 homers in a season twice. And no NL player would top that single-season mark for nearly 50 years.

Kiner was traded to the Chicago Cubs in 1953. That same season, the Pirates took their first steps toward desegregating their roster. This was just six years after Jackie Robinson's debut with the Brooklyn Dodgers, breaking the color barrier in Major League Baseball (MLB), and many teams still had segregated rosters.

The Pirates called up minor leaguer outfielder Carlos Bernier, a native of Puerto Rico. He spent just one year with the Pirates. In 1954 second baseman Curt Roberts joined the Pirates. Roberts had spent four years with the Kansas City Monarchs of the Negro Leagues.

Pirates slugger Ralph Kiner led the majors in home runs in six of his eight seasons in Pittsburgh.

Bernier and Roberts didn't have much of an impact on the field. But they paved the way for the arrival of perhaps the greatest Pirate of them all. On April 17, 1955, Pittsburgh hosted the Dodgers in a doubleheader. Roberto Clemente, a 20-year-old outfielder, also from Puerto Rico, was penciled into the Pirates' lineup batting third and playing right field. Clemente singled in his first major league at-bat and added two hits, including a double, in the second game.

Clemente's early years weren't all so smooth. Early on the Spanish-speaking player struggled with speaking a different language than his teammates. He also had to learn how to hit major league pitches. But as the decade came to a close, Clemente was on his way to becoming one of MLB's first Latin American stars. And with their star outfielder leading the way, the Pirates were on the way to something big.

HARD-LUCK HARVEY

On May 26, 1959, Pirates lefty Harvey Haddix had one of the best—and worst—days imaginable at the ballpark. Facing the Braves in Milwaukee, the 33-year-old journeyman pitched 12 perfect innings. Despite retiring 36 straight batters, Haddix continued, because the Pirates hadn't scored a run. Finally in the 13th inning, a Braves hitter reached on an error. Three batters later, Haddix gave up a double and Pittsburgh lost 1–0.

CHAPTER 3

A SERIES TO REMEMBER

The sun was shining and a warm breeze blew through Forbes Field on October 13, 1960. Though autumn had arrived three weeks earlier, Pittsburgh was getting at least one more day of summer weather. That was fitting, because the Pirates and New York Yankees were about to play the last game of the baseball season.

The 1960 World Series had reached Game 7 in an unusual fashion. The Yankees had just won their 11th AL pennant in 14 years. Eight of those seasons ended in World Series victories for the Bronx Bombers of New York. And their experience showed against the young Pirates, who hadn't reached the World Series since 1927. Over the first six games, the Yankees outscored

Pittsburgh ace Vernon Law pitches during Game 7 of the 1960 World Series against the New York Yankees.

Pittsburgh 46–17. But New York had won three blowouts—16–3, 10–0, and 12–0—while the Pirates had won three close games.

Still, the Pirates felt confident heading into Game 7. They had their ace Vernon Law on the mound. He was that year's Cy Young Award winner as baseball's top pitcher. And he'd already posted victories in Game 1 and Game 4. Meanwhile, the Yankees had already used their best pitcher, Whitey Ford, to win Game 6. That meant he wouldn't be available for the clincher. More than 36,000 fans crammed into Forbes Field to witness what some would later call the greatest game in MLB history.

The Pirates jumped on Yankees starter Bob Turley and one reliever to take a 4–0 lead into the fifth. However, the drama was just beginning. Law, who had been troubled by a sore ankle, gave up a home run to Bill Skowron in the fifth. In the sixth, Pirates manager Danny Murtaugh turned to his top reliever, Roy Face. The veteran right-hander had won an amazing 18 games out of the bullpen in 1959, and in 1960, he posted 10 wins and 24 saves. Face had closed out all three Pirates victories in the series. But the Yankees were ready for him in Game 7. Law allowed the first two batters to reach base. Then Face came in to retire his first batter, but he gave up a single to Mickey Mantle. After that Yogi Berra's three-run homer capped a four-run rally.

New York put together another rally in the eighth, when a walk and three straight hits produced two more runs. The Yankees took a 7–4 lead into the bottom of the eighth. They appeared to be on their way to yet another title.

COMEBACK TIME

Instead, the Pirates fought back. Three straight hits delivered a run. With two outs, Roberto Clemente's infield single scored another run, cutting the Yankees' lead to 7–6. Suddenly, Forbes Field had come alive. Then the crowd erupted when backup catcher Hal Smith launched a three-run homer over the left-field fence. The five-run eighth inning left Pittsburgh three outs away from winning the World Series.

But the Yankees rallied again, scratching out two runs to tie the game 9–9. Pittsburgh second baseman Bill Mazeroski was scheduled to lead off the bottom of the ninth. He later

Danny Murtaugh led the Pirates to World Series championships in 1960 and 1971 during his 15 years as manager.

Pirates second baseman Bill Mazeroski is mobbed by his teammates and fans after his walk-off home run to win the 1960 World Series.

said that he was so stunned by the Yankees' comeback that someone on his team had to remind him he was up first.

It didn't take long for Mazeroski to write his name into the history books. On Ralph Terry's second pitch, Mazeroski blasted a high fly ball to left. The Yankees outfielders could only watch as it carried over the ivy-covered fence for a walk-off home run. Mazeroski waved his helmet as he sprinted around the bases. Fans streamed onto the field to celebrate. When Mazeroski reached home plate, he was mobbed by teammates and spectators alike. One of the most dramatic home runs in MLB history gave the Pirates a 10–9 win and another World Series title.

CLEMENTE RISES

The Pirates didn't return to the postseason in the 1960s, but Clemente emerged as one of the best players in the world during that time. He led all MLB players with 1,877 hits during the decade. Clemente was the NL Most Valuable Player (MVP) in 1966, and the next season he won his fourth batting title with a career-high .357 average. He also used his speed and powerful arm to win 12 straight Gold Glove Awards as one of the NL's best fielding outfielders. Opponents quickly learned not to try to take an extra base when Clemente was in the lineup.

By the dawn of the 1970s, Clemente was the elder role model on a Pittsburgh team facing a lot of changes. The first was decided by the league. MLB split the AL and NL into East and West divisions in 1969, and the new arrangement suited the Pirates well. They won six NL East titles in the 1970s, and two of those teams played memorable series deep into October.

KEEPING THE FAITH

Every year on October 13, fans honor the anniversary of the Pirates' Game 7 victory over the Yankees in 1960. They gather at the site of old Forbes Field to relive one of the team's greatest moments. They listen to radio replays and watch video of the game. And every year, they replay Bill Mazeroski's home run at precisely 3:36 p.m.—the same time he hit it on that warm fall afternoon in 1960.

Three Rivers Stadium was home to the Pirates from 1970 to 2000.

On July 16, 1970, the Pirates played their first home game at Three Rivers Stadium. Forbes Field had served them well for more than 60 seasons, but new ballparks were springing up all over the country. Like many others, Pittsburgh's was a multipurpose stadium, meaning it also hosted football games and other events. Three Rivers Stadium also featured a smaller outfield with the fences closer to home plate than those at Forbes Field.

The 1971 squad was the first to play a full season at Three Rivers, and left fielder Willie Stargell was the first to take advantage of the closer fences. He led the majors with 48 home runs that season as the Pirates cruised to the NL East title.

In the NL Championship Series (NLCS), the Pirates defeated the San Francisco Giants three games to one. That sent Pittsburgh back to the World Series for the first time in 11 years. The defending champion Baltimore Orioles awaited. The Orioles had everything—power, speed, defense, and especially pitching, with four 20-game winners on the staff that year. However, the Pirates had Clemente. He used the series to remind baseball fans of his greatness, even at age 37.

The teams split the first six games, with the home team winning each of them. Game 7 was slated for Baltimore's Memorial Stadium. Clemente got the Pirates on the board first, blasting a hanging curveball from Mike Cuellar over the fence in left-center in the fourth inning. He jogged around the bases with his arms loose, looking like a man who knew he'd just won the World Series.

It helped that Pirates starter Steve Blass had put the clamps on the Orioles' high-flying offense. Blass scattered four hits

Hall of Fame outfielder Roberto Clemente steps into his swing during the 1971 World Series against the Baltimore Orioles.

and walked two over nine strong innings. His teammates added a second run in the eighth on José Pagán's RBI double. The Orioles scratched out a run in the bottom of the eighth, but that was all Blass would give them.

With two outs in the bottom of the ninth, Pirates shortstop Jackie Hernández fielded a ground ball up the middle. He fired it to first baseman Bob Robertson, and the game was over. Blass sprinted toward first base and jumped into Robertson's arms. The Pirates were world champions.

Clemente hit .414 with five extra-base hits, including two home runs, over the seven games. He was named World Series MVP for his efforts. Sadly, it would be the final major award of his career. Clemente collected his 3,000th career hit on his last regular season at-bat of the 1972 season. Then, tragedy struck.

Though he was from Puerto Rico, Clemente was a hero throughout Latin America. People admired his dedication to helping others in the region. In December 1972, a massive earthquake struck in Nicaragua. Clemente, who was playing winter ball in Puerto Rico, led efforts to raise money and provide supplies for the victims.

However, he heard rumors that the Nicaraguan army had stolen the first shipment that was meant to help the citizens. So he decided he would fly to Nicaragua with the next shipment on December 31 to make sure it wasn't taken. But he never made it. The plane crashed just off the coast of Puerto Rico, killing everyone on board. The news stunned the baseball community, which quickly went about honoring the legendary player. The Pirates retired his number, and the Baseball Hall of Fame waived its five-year waiting period to induct him the next year.

Pirates fans were heartbroken. There would never be another like Clemente, whose skills on the field were matched by his integrity off it. The fans wouldn't have to wait long, however, to cheer for another winner.

CHAPTER 4

FAMILY AND THE FUTURE

The 1979 season started with a whimper for the Pirates. They stumbled out of the gate, losing 10 of their first 14 games. In late May, nearly a quarter of the way through the season, they were still just 18–21. They trailed the first-place Montreal Expos by seven games in the NL East.

The Pirates were expected to contend for the NL pennant that year. The pitching staff was strong. Pittsburgh's starting rotation featured lefty John Candelaria and right-handers Bert Blyleven and Bruce Kison, all in their prime. Closer Kent Tekulve led a deep and experienced bullpen. And the offensive attack was dangerous. Though nearing age 40, Willie Stargell was still a power threat. So was burly right fielder Dave Parker, the 1978

Pirates first baseman and unofficial captain Willie Stargell takes off toward first after his hit at Three Rivers Stadium in 1979.

NL MVP. And speedy center fielder Omar Moreno was a terror on the base paths.

It felt like just a matter of time before the Pirates put it all together. Stargell, the unofficial captain, thought the team needed something to rally around. Then, on June 1, it came to him. During a rain delay at Three Rivers Stadium, the speakers blared popular music to keep the fans entertained. One song caught Stargell's attention: "We Are Family" by Sister Sledge.

The song was upbeat and fun. And it emphasized the benefits of sticking together and relying on each other. Stargell declared it the team's official song. Both players and fans embraced it. The song played throughout the stadium during games. Eventually, it even replaced "Take Me Out to the Ball Game" during the seventh-inning stretch at Three Rivers. That summer, the Family was the story in Pittsburgh.

On the field, the Pirates made another big change. They traded for third baseman Bill Madlock. Already a two-time NL batting champion, Madlock would hit

POPS

Willie "Pops" Stargell spent his entire 21-year major league career with the Pirates. The seven-time All-Star was one of baseball's most feared power hitters. And he was the team's spiritual leader. He awarded "Stargell Stars" to teammates who had made a big play or had a great game. In 1979, at age 39, he became the first player to win the MVP awards for the regular season, NLCS, and World Series.

.328 the rest of the season and deepened an already strong lineup.

Whether it was Madlock or the song, the Pirates caught fire in the second half. On July 8, they won the second half of a doubleheader against the Reds in Cincinnati. That was the first of 13 wins in their next 14 games. The Pirates started the streak in fourth place, seven games out of first. By the end, they were in second place, just a game behind the Expos.

Pirates third baseman Bill Madlock looks to make a throw to first during the 1979 season.

Pittsburgh rode that momentum the rest of the way. It posted a 52–25 record after the All-Star Game and clinched the division title on the last day of the season. Facing the Reds in the NLCS, it won the first two games on the road in extra innings. Then it completed the three-game sweep with a 7–1 win back at home.

The 1979 World Series was a rematch with the Baltimore Orioles. It looked like the Orioles were set on getting revenge for their loss to Pittsburgh in 1971, as they took three of the first four games. But with their backs to the wall, the Pirates rallied for seven runs in their final three at-bats to take Game 5. Candelaria and Tekulve then combined on a shutout in Game 6, meaning the World Series would again come down to one game.

The Orioles led 1–0 in the top of the sixth when the leader of the Family took center stage. First Bill Robinson reached on a bad-hop single with one out. Then Stargell drove Scott McGregor's first pitch deep into the Baltimore night. The two-run homer turned out to be the winning blow. Pittsburgh tacked on two more runs in the ninth, and Tekulve took care of the final three outs. The Pirates celebrated their fifth World Series title in team history and second against the Orioles.

BARRY AND THE BOYS

Stargell hung on for three more injury-riddled seasons before retiring in 1982. The Pirates went through some tough times in the 1980s, including a 104-loss season in 1985. But they soon began a successful rebuilding phase, stacking the roster with a number of young, talented players. First among them was Barry Bonds.

Barry Bonds made his MLB debut with the Pirates in 1986.

Left fielder Bonds, the Pirates' first-round pick in the 1985 draft, was called up in May of the 1986 season. The Pirates also made several smart trades over the next two years. They acquired third baseman Bobby Bonilla, center fielder Andy Van Slyke, and pitcher Doug Drabek. By 1990 those four formed the core of a team that would win the next three NL East titles.

BARRY BONDS

Barry Bonds is one of the more controversial figures in baseball history. He won the NL MVP Award in 1990 and 1992 for his elite combination of power, speed, and defense. But he also feuded with teammates and management. He left as a free agent, signing with the San Francisco Giants in 1993. He won five more MVP trophies there and went on to break the MLB single-season and career home run records. But he also was suspected of using performance-enhancing drugs, which will forever taint his legacy.

However, each year their luck ran out in the NLCS. In 1990 they lost to the eventual World Series champion Reds in six games. In 1991 they returned to Pittsburgh with a 3–2 series lead against the Atlanta Braves. They needed just one win to finish off the series. Instead, Atlanta's outstanding young pitching staff tossed two shutouts to crush the Pirates' hopes.

The 1992 NLCS might have been the most painful of all. Trailing the Braves three games to one, the Pirates won two straight to force Game 7. Then they took a 2–0 lead into the

PNC Park is one of baseball's most scenic stadiums, with views of the downtown skyline and the Allegheny riverfront.

bottom of the ninth. Needing just three outs to reach the World Series, the roof caved in. Atlanta rallied for three runs, the last two scoring on a bases-loaded single with two outs.

That spelled the end of the Pirates' reign in the NL. The team's owners decided to trim their payroll and focus on building with younger, cheaper players. The results were disastrous. Most of the young players weren't good enough

Pirates center fielder Andrew McCutchen slides to make a play in a 2013 game against the Cincinnati Reds at PNC Park.

to help the team improve. The Pirates signed free agents who didn't produce. And they made trades that usually worked out better for the other side. From 1993 to 2012, the Pirates averaged just 69 wins per year and finished 13 or more games out of first every year but one.

The major highlight of that era came in 2001. That's when the Pirates moved into PNC Park. Their sparkling new

ballpark in downtown
Pittsburgh drew rave
reviews from fans and
players. The owners just
had a hard time putting
a winning team on
the field to match the
wonderful surroundings.

Finally, in 2013, the
Pirates resurfaced in the
postseason. They were led
by center fielder Andrew
McCutchen. He was one of
the most exciting players
in the major leagues. He
made great plays in the
outfield and came up with huge hits all season. McCutchen
won the NL MVP Award and led Pittsburgh to at 94-win season
and an NL wild-card spot. It was the first of three straight
wild-card berths for the Pirates. Although they only advanced
to the Division Series once, fans saw it as a sign that Pittsburgh
could build a winning team. The rest of the decade was filled
with more struggles, but hopes ran high that the next great era
of Pirates baseball might be just around the corner.

Pirates players celebrate after their
10th-inning walk-off win over the
Chicago Cubs at PNC Park during
the 2022 season.

TIMELINE

1882

The Pittsburgh Alleghenys join the American Association.

1887

The Alleghenys jump to the National League. They change their nickname to the Pirates four years later.

1900

Former Louisville owner Barney Dreyfuss buys the Pirates and brings 14 players with him to Pittsburgh, including future Hall of Famers Honus Wagner and Fred Clarke.

1903

The Boston Americans defeat the Pirates five games to three in the first World Series.

1909

The Pirates move into Forbes Field in June. Four months later, they win their first World Series, defeating Ty Cobb and the Detroit Tigers four games to three.

1925

Pittsburgh returns to the World Series and defeats the Washington Senators in seven games.

1946

Rookie outfielder Ralph Kiner wins the first of seven straight NL home run crowns.

1960

On October 13, Bill Mazeroski hits a walk-off homer to lift the Pirates over the Yankees in Game 7 of the World Series.

1967

Roberto Clemente wins his fourth NL batting title and is named the NL MVP.

1970

Three Rivers Stadium opens. It will be the home of the Pirates and Pittsburgh Steelers for the next 30 seasons.

1971

The Pirates win a thrilling seven-game World Series against the Baltimore Orioles.

1972

On December 31, Clemente is killed in a plane crash while delivering relief supplies to earthquake victims in Nicaragua.

1979

Willie Stargell becomes the first player to be named MVP of the regular season, NLCS, and World Series as the Pirates again beat the Orioles in seven games to win their fifth title.

1992

The Atlanta Braves score three runs in the ninth to win Game 7 and advance to the World Series, handing the Pirates their third straight NLCS defeat.

2001

The Pirates move into PNC Park.

2013

Andrew McCutchen wins the NL MVP Award and leads the Pirates to the first of three straight NL wild-card berths.

TEAM FACTS

FRANCHISE HISTORY

Pittsburgh Alleghenys
  (1882–90)
Pittsburgh Pirates (1891–)

WORLD SERIES CHAMPIONSHIPS

1909, 1925, 1960, 1971, 1979

KEY PLAYERS

Barry Bonds (1986–92)
Max Carey (1910–26)
Roberto Clemente (1955–72)
Doug Drabek (1987–92)
Ralph Kiner (1946–53)
Bill Mazeroski (1956–72)
Andrew McCutchen (2009–17)
Dave Parker (1973–83)
Willie Stargell (1962–82)
Arky Vaughan (1932–41)
Honus Wagner (1900–17)
Paul Waner (1926–40)

KEY MANAGERS

Fred Clarke (1900–15)
Jim Leyland (1986–96)
Danny Murtaugh (1957–64,
  1967, 1970–71, 1973–76)
Chuck Tanner (1977–85)

HOME STADIUMS

Exposition Park I (1882–1883)
Exposition Park II (1883)
Recreation Park (1884–1890)
Exposition Park III (1891–1909)
Forbes Field (1909–1970)
Three Rivers Stadium
  (1970–2000)
PNC Park (2001–)

TEAM TRIVIA

FAMOUS LAST BLAST

Forbes Field was the site of Babe Ruth's final career home run on May 25, 1935. Ruth's 714th homer stood as a career record until 1974. He was playing for the Boston Braves. The blast cleared the 86-foot (26 m) high roof in right field.

POWER SURGE

In May 1956, Pirates first baseman Dale Long set a record by hitting home runs in eight straight games. The record would later be tied by the Yankees' Don Mattingly in 1987 and Ken Griffey Jr. of the Seattle Mariners in 1993.

LUCKY SEVENS

On September 16, 1975, the Pirates beat the Chicago Cubs 22–0. Pittsburgh second baseman Rennie Stennett went 7-for-7 on the day—four singles, two doubles, and a triple. That made him the first player in the modern era to collect seven hits in a nine-inning game.

SECRET HONOR

The right-field fence at PNC Park is 21 feet high (6.4 m). That was intentional—it was designed to honor Roberto Clemente, the former right fielder whose No. 21 was retired by the Pirates.

GLOSSARY

ace

A team's best starting pitcher.

bullpen

The place where relief pitchers warm up; also used to refer to a team's relievers as a group.

closer

A pitcher who comes in at the end of the game to secure a win for his team.

free agent

A player whose rights are not owned by any team.

ground-rule double

A ball that hits in fair territory beyond the infield and bounces out of play; the batter is awarded two bases.

journeyman

A player who has played for many teams or has been unable to find a specific role.

pennant

Another name for a league championship; in MLB, refers to winning either the American or National League.

save

When a relief pitcher comes into a close game and preserves a win.

segregate

To separate groups of people based on race, gender, ethnicity, or other factors.

shutout

A complete game in which a team allows no runs.

walk-off home run

A home run in the final inning that wins the game for the home team, forcing the defense to walk off the field.

MORE INFORMATION

BOOKS

Flynn, Brendan. *The MLB Encyclopedia*. Minneapolis, MN: Abdo Publishing, 2022.

Harris, Duchess, JD, PhD, with Alex Kies. *The Negro Leagues*. Minneapolis, MN: Abdo Publishing, 2020.

Hewson, Anthony K. *GOATs of Baseball*. Minneapolis, MN: Abdo Publishing, 2022.

ONLINE RESOURCES

To learn more about the Pittsburgh Pirates, visit **abdobooklinks.com** or scan this QR code. These links are routinely monitored and updated to provide the most current information available.

INDEX

ABOUT THE AUTHOR

Patrick Donnelly is a freelance writer who lives in Minneapolis, Minnesota. He has covered Major League Baseball for more than 20 years.